Love Blossom

Vanessa Dehn

BookLeaf
Publishing

India | USA | UK

Presentation by *BookLeaf Publishing*

Web: www.bookleafpub.com

E-mail: info@bookleafpub.com

ISBN : 9789357447294

First edition 2021

DEDICATION

This is for you, as always.

ACKNOWLEDGEMENT

First of all, I want to thank you for spending your time reading the words I was writing for you. Thank you for reading and listening to yourself.

I thank everyone who is part of my poetry journey and supported me with feedback. There is my dear friend, you are part of this journey from the real beginning. Thank you for diving deep into my world and encouraging me to write this book. Your creativity is such an inspiration to me. There is my twin sister. You were always believing in me and in my poems. Thank you so much for your love - a love which cannot be stronger than this. I want to thank my mom for listening and inspiring me many many times. I often feel that I could write through you. Thank you for being my mother and for your love which is so unique, pure and unconditional. There is my wonderful partner - I couldn't ask for a better one. You are such an inspiration to me and your love can be found in my words. And lastly, I thank myself to let in all the kinds of love.

The seed

And suddenly I woke up
and realized that my own cup
was empty and cold,
for a long time disguised
with plenty of mold.
But after a single decision
and a couple revisions,
the cup was accessible again.
To fill it with love and let the rain from above
water the seed
which was planted inside
to grow inner love
from ebb to flood tide.

Always is almost always a not always

always feels oddly out of all ways
but love seems to be in some ways always
or rather in most of all ways
which leads me to the assumption
that my love for you is almost not-always.

Symphony

Sometimes in some nights
I surreptitiously put myself in your dreams
to be a part of your symmetry
that is a symphony in every single segment
and I would lie if I said it happens seldomly.

Between sunlight and satisfaction

I am somewhere between sunlight and
satisfaction.
Your spicy soul just touched mine slightly.
It is soothing to get along with such a
serendipity,
somewhere in between but intertwined.

Twin Love

You are me and not me.
I am you and not you.
Two individuals, two separate parts that live in
one another.
And when I'm with you I just feel complete.
On the deepest level one can imagine.

Mirroring

I see, you see
just the reflection as it should be.
The light gives a virtual idea;
but you see, I see what I want to be.

You and me - two individuals

you and me - two individual poles;
attracted by adoration,
degaussed by missing infatuation,
repelled by lack of compassion.
What remains is you and me - two individual
poles.

Love in the moment

Our love is just peripheral
like the smoke of a candle - ephemeral.
What remains is the evanescence
that makes this instant of time eternal.

What is my calling?

Due to the force of gravity
the planet is attracting me.
I'm standing stable, I am not falling
but if I fall, then into my calling.

But what's the answer to the question of who I
am?
What's the question to the answer, "I am not?"
Am I a dancer of life or less than a lot?
I try to listen to myself, but I cannot.
I cannot hear what's in my heart, what's in my
soul
What is the mission, what is the goal?

What is the purpose of living on earth?
Birth and death, and death and birth.
Hidden feelings and emotions
which are deeper than the oceans

And sometimes I feel stuck.
Stuck in this wrong construct
of my own reality
created out of the duality
of my thoughts.

So I'm standing stable but I feel lost.
Without connection to my roots
ready to recruit
my inner soldiers to build my army
to fight against my harmony.

But I feel weaker instead of stronger
so I don't want to fight any longer
so I put the weapons to the ground
and listen to my heart beating sound.

I'm alive. I'm here.
And facing my deepest fear
let me realize that living and existing are not the
same
let me realize there is a higher aim in this game.

And in this greatest hour,
I remember who I am.
And I awaken all my power
and see how powerful I am.

And I realize, I am the creator of my own life.
I am the manifest of my grown child.
I feel connected to my wild side
and experience that I shine bright.

And within this single verse,

sending a signal to the universe
I'm not alone on our earth,
I feel home and I feel worth.

I start with installing
all the new things I've learned.

But the question that's still in my head is
What is my calling,
what can I spread?

And the answer could be: expressing myself
in my truest version, in my truest self.
And I start to feel the love for myself
With the deepest love I have ever felt.

And if you feel lost and like you could fall,
please remember your power which flows in us
all.

From zenith to setting

Hand in hand,
we draw our circles
along the coast.
The ocean beats its waves,
from diffraction to interference.
The moon - from zenith to setting.
Just you and me on this summer night
and I know it's just right.

Love loves

I feel this inner force
down at the bottom of my heart.
It leads me back to the course
saves me from being apart.
A connection, an affective memory,
a deeper meaning in my story.
This is it, this is love
and it loves to make me feel loved.

Phantasmagoria

I was drowning in your delusive smile
until I popped up in my own reality.
What I've seen in you
is a deception after a disenchantment.
Just an unfolded illustration of my fantasy - a
phantasmagoria.

Love in every single day

I remember it was a Monday when I
had this mellow melodic tune in my mind.
On a Tuesday, I knew it was time to turn it into
a takeoff tune.
I start wandering on a Wednesday,
finally traveling towards you on that tasteful
Thursday.
I remember your friendly face on that
flamboyant Friday
and I can tell special stories on Saturdays and
stealing another sweet smile from you on
Sundays.

The burgeon

My love, it's time to burgeon.
The feeling inside is where to converge in.
Just close your eyes and lean in,
the love will arise and is seen then
in your inner eye; my love
now is the time to fly.

Mis-taken chances

We can escape from all the might-have-beens
and the concept of everything is possible
and turn them into taken chances and lived
possibilities.
But before I take you by the hand I have to ask -
are you brave enough to follow?

Ineffable but writable

And sometimes someone makes you
unable to find
words for your inner world.
And from wonder
you start to ponder
until you accept
that love is ineffable.

With everything I am

Whenever I get close enough
I promise to look at you
with everything I have.
Whenever I promise enough
I close my eyes to look at you
while having everything I want.

Autumn Love

From a stranger I barely know
to a friend whom I allow
to touch my heart very slowly,
to live, to love, to smile and to grow;
to dance in the autumn rain
and tell the world I am yours
but I am still mine.

The Love within

I was falling - into my heart.
Now I am floating 'cause I carry myself.

Love and Life - love and live

Love is when fantasy becomes real
and reality feels fantastic.

Life is when emotions are felt
and feelings are in motion.

The blossom

I remembered all my colours
that make life so wonderfully colourful and
unique.
This inner strength led me there to break down
the dreary grey into its colourful components.
And I know that I never want to go back.
Because as of today, the blossom has awakened.

www.ingramcontent.com/pod-product-compliance
Lightning Source LLC
LaVergne TN
LVHW050249200726

843509LV00015B/2958